The

Eternity

Principle

Glenn Thomas Carson

Forever & ever —

[signature]

POLAR STAR PRESS°
✝ ·

For information, write Disciples of Christ Historical Society, 1101 19th Ave., S., Nashville, TN 37212

FIRST EDITION

Polar Star Press, the Three Streams Cross (with The Future of History), and The Place History Calls Home are Trademarks of Disciples of Christ Historical Society, Nashville, Tennessee, USA, and Registered in the U.S. Patent and Trademark Office

ISBN 978-0-980196-4-1

12   24   17   72

To

The Memories of

William Thomas Carson
(my Dad)

John Eben Carson
(my brother)

Willeen Carson Burke
(my sister)

Douglas Eugene Briscoe
(my mentor)

All live now in Eternity

All quotations of Scripture
have been translated
and/or paraphrased
by the author.

This book is intended for
the devotional reader
and is not a work of
technical theology.

God is beyond gender.
However, for ease of reading,
'he' is sometimes used here

Table of Contents

*Eternity
Is
Real*

Prologue

I have always been fascinated by the idea of eternity. As a child, growing up in conservative Protestantism, I was told that not only was the existence of eternity factual, but that personal choice determined whether it would be a pleasant, or quite unpleasant, experience. Forever and ever.

Since then I have learned, among other things, that truth and fact do not always coincide. And I have learned that 'eternity' is much too big a concept for any of us mere humans to fully grasp.

The idea of eternity has intrigued all of us for at least as long as we have been writing things down. And we have been here much longer than that. The earth and the universe it spins in have been here much longer still. We cannot really fathom these eons of time, so it is no wonder that we have little understanding of that 'place' lying outside the realm of time and space. This lack of understanding does not make the idea any less intriguing, but it does lead us back to a rightful measure of humility.

I am a person of faith and live out my hope and expectation within the Christian Church (Disciples of

Christ). I am also a true ecumenist. It is not my intention, then, for anything in these pages to communicate exclusivity. Nor do I wish to convey that I somehow, suddenly, have all the answers. None of us do.

Traditional language and images are used here to facilitate understanding, but not, I hope, in a limiting way. This book is the result of my ongoing wonder at this marvelous world we inhabit. Far from having the answers, I think of more questions with each passing year. Perhaps something here will help you consider your questions in a new way. And then you can form your own answers to this timeless notion called eternity.

GTC

No longer time...
but eternity

~ St. Augustine ~

Book One
Time and Eternity

The Eternity Principle

Eternity is real. It is an actual place. There are many people, perhaps, who think of eternity as an idea, or simply wishful thinking. But imagine for a moment: What if it were more than an idea? What if the concept of a spiritual dimension called eternity was more than a wish? What if, instead, it was another dimension parallel to our own? A dimension not made of space and time like the one in which we exist, but one made of spirit and timelessness. Not just a philosophical notion, but an actual place where persons live and work and create.

That is the point of this book. Eternity is literally an invisible realm where spiritual persons live and function and carry on meaningful discourse. But the book has a further point: You can become a citizen of this spiritual realm. You have the ability right now to choose to become a spiritual person and join the citizenry of eternity. Through the activation of what I call the **Eternity Principle**, you can begin living now in eternity, while continuing with your life here. You are already a citizen in our physical world of time and space. You can choose dual citizenship, however, and enter the realm of timelessness at any moment.

What is this principle that allows you to leap from the limitations of time to the boundlessness of eternity? It is a simple concept that, once understood, will radically alter your experience as a human being. Suddenly you will see yourself more clearly, you will understand the world around you with more clarity, and you will be able to reach beyond where you are to where God is. It is a principle that allows you to move from the merely natural to the supernatural in a way that is both objectively real and personally meaningful.

Simply put:

The Eternity Principle is the power of God at work in you.

Let's explore this wonderful idea together. In doing so, we will learn about God, about ourselves, and about how we can join with him to create a better place to live – now and in eternity.

Dimension and Form

There is eternal energy which is the source of all life. It has its genesis in the eternal dimension, but it nonetheless pulses through our own dimension giving form and structure to our physical universe. Like electricity, it is an invisible force, but it is infinitely more potent. And here is the wonderful secret: spiritual power (which is eternal) can be used in the material world (which is temporal). You can tap into the eternal realm and use its power to solve problems of emotion, relationship, economics, and spirit. God's power is available for you and by contacting him you also connect with the universal power that can re-create you into a complete person.

God's main interest is for you to become a total human being. He is a spiritual person, who is concerned with you, too, becoming a spiritual person. And isn't that your ultimate goal really? Don't you long to become a person with more discipline, a more loving attitude, and an unclouded vision for your personal future? In fact, don't you wish you were more spiritually aware than you are right now? It is possible and that is the marvel of the Eternity Principle.

But I will not present eternity and its power in some vague, generic form that has no intellectual handles to grasp. Instead, I will point to the personal, relational nature of eternity and show you how the gateway from your visible world to the invisible world is relationship. While there are facts and principles involved – it is, after all, the Eternity **Principle** – the whole idea of eternity, with its divine power, is established on intimate relationship.

That is why I am a Christian. If your goal is to reach eternity and to touch God, then the historic facts and personal faith of Christianity can help you reach that goal in a very meaningful way. The reason is simple: Christianity is not in the main a religion about ritual and ceremony and holy days. It is, instead, a religion about becoming personally connected with God. Christianity offers a unique view into the nature of God. It is a personal religion, based on relationship. So, Christianity offers a contrast between the outward and the inward; the ceremonial and the real; the ritualistic and the relational.

Eternity is a dimension inhabited by spiritual persons and contact between persons requires relationship. The Eternity Principle, finally, does not just offer you eternal power, not even just eternity itself, but the opportunity to reach beyond yourself and develop a one-on-one relationship with God.

Jesus of Nazareth made a radical shift in the definition of religion. In his first century world, religion was primarily understood as ritualistic performance for the appeasement of God or gods. In other words, people believed that in order to contact the eternal, they had to carry out certain ceremonies, reciting particular liturgy. Through the ritual, or ceremony, it was believed that individuals (or nations) could attain prosperity, happiness, peace, and ultimately immortality. The proper execution of the ceremonies themselves, it was thought, pleased the gods, who then granted favor to mortal human beings.

But Jesus changed all that.

He understood that sacrament only portrays relationship. Sacrament is only a representation (or symbol) of reality. The reality is the relationship that can exist between spiritual persons. This does not discount the importance of the symbol. In baptism, for example, we see the new purity within by the sign of pure baptismal water. We are witnesses to the new bond that the believer has with God and with the community of faith. But the point that Christ made is that while this kind of symbol is important and it has meaning, it is, nonetheless, a symbol and only represents a deeper reality.

The Christian religion presents the possibility of up-close, personal, intimate contact between humanity and divinity. Jesus taught that ritual was secondary to the primary purpose of contact with eternity. And, in fact, he also shifted the understanding of that primary purpose, as well.

The reason that a person should connect with eternity, Jesus believed, was not first and foremost in order to gain some kind of divine power, or the right to inherit immortality. Instead, a personal relationship was offered by God. He has reached out to you and to me and desires for us to reach out to him. It is not just contact with divine energy. It is a relationship with God himself. Jesus saw clearly that human beings had the capacity for union with God. And then, a by-product of that relationship is inner peace, purpose for living, and spiritual power. In short, we can have it all – a relationship with the Creator of the universe and the eternal, internal power to live through our present circumstances and to literally live forever.

Marcus Aurelius, in his ancient *Meditations*, proclaimed: *As you intend to live hereafter, it is in your power to live here.* In other words, you do not have to wait for a future after-life to begin the proccss of becoming a complete, total human being. You intend to become a person of perfection in eternity, Aurelius would say, but you actually have the capacity for some level of perfection here and now.

With that knowledge, of course, comes the cancellation of all excuses. We can no longer point to some unknown date in the future and declare that **then** will be the time to begin truly living. All excuses are off. We intend to live full, complete lives in eternity and we have within us the power to reach for perfection in this life. Just as we are in the process of completion here in the world of time and space, we will continue the process of completion in the world of timelessness. The process of becoming a whole person will never end. You intend to grow spiritually and emotionally and intellectually in this life and you will continue to grow in these ways in eternity. Eternity means life in its essence; and life never stops growing and becoming and processing.

So, the power to live – to truly live – already resides within you. All you have to do is choose life. And you can do that by activating the Eternity Principle.

I began this book by saying that eternity is real. You either believe that already or are at least interested in the idea, or you would not be reading this right now. It is my conviction, though, that the reality of eternity must transcend our own thoughts about it. It must be objectively real apart from our own conceptions of it. Because if it isn't, then it is just wishful thinking after all.

I hope, then, that by coming to understand the Eternity Principle, you will come to better comprehend eternity itself. And maybe along the way, you will envision a more complete picture of yourself and your world, and how you can make a lasting difference. Maybe even an eternal difference.

Death and Life

Are we truly temporary creatures? By virtue of our biological natures we exist for a relatively short period of time. In terms of human history, the life-span of any one individual is so short that it could be considered inconsequential. In comparison to the millennia upon millennia that the planet has existed, the shortness of an individual human life is almost immeasurable. We are physical, biological beings who live temporarily within transient cultures.

Since we know all of this to be true, how can we rationally speak of timelessness, or eternity? The earth is ever-changing. Humanity is a constantly transmuting mass of faces, which forever remains the same in the midst of unceasing change. In the midst of this temporary system, some people feel compelled to proclaim the very real possibility of eternity. It is what I call the Eternity Principle. But if, indeed, eternity is real, then how does it affect us and in what ways do we interact with it?

God actually exists in eternity. That is, he is not limited, as we are, by the dimensions of time and space. He is not a physical, biological being. He is a spiritual person and lives in a dimension distinct from our own.

The amazing fact, though, and one which is difficult for us to accept because of our limitations, is that God can reach out from his spiritual world into our physical world. He is able to translate himself – spiritually – into our sphere which is not in the main spiritual. In so doing, he communicates with us and offers us the opportunity to glimpse into eternity.

The Eternity Principle, then, is the activation of God's Spirit within us so that the eternal becomes as real for us as the temporal. It is a principle charged by the powerful force that created the universe, so that its precepts carry to the inner most part of our beings an ability to literally see into the other dimension.

Evidence of this principle is found throughout the New Testament. In the Gospels, Jesus continually points to the connection between eternal and temporal; spiritual and physical. To the Samaritan woman (John 4) he explains that God is a spiritual person. *God is spirit*, Jesus says, *and must be related to in spirit and in truth*. But how can we, living within this physical dimension, relate to God (worship) in a spiritual way? If there is no interrelatedness between the eternal and temporal realms, then Christ was only using metaphoric language to express religious wishful-thinking. If, on the other hand, the two dimensions are somehow connected, then he is speaking plainly about a very real spiritual relationship that is possible with God.

The first part of Christ's proposition is simple enough: God is a spiritual person. That is, he is not a human being with the confinements of body, space, and time. He is an eternal person who lives beyond the entrapment of physicality. What Jesus is saying is that God actually lives in another dimension. It is a dimension that we humans can communicate with, as we will see, but it is nonetheless a separate and distinct place.

The second part of the declaration is not as easily deciphered. Jesus asserts that those who wish to worship God must do so *in spirit*. Now, if there were no chance of connecting with the eternal dimension in which God lives, it would be impossible to carry out this demand. If we are totally limited by space, time, and biology, then it is futile to attempt contact with a spiritual God. But, if in fact we can relate to God in a spiritual way, then the borders between our dimension and God's dimension are not un-crossable and may actually overlap to form a sort of "spiritual zone" where true communion between divine and human is possible.

The Samaritan woman did not at first believe Christ's message. She was so bound by her natural dimension of space and time that she was convinced (like many others) that God could only be contacted in a specific (physical) place. Some in the New Testament era would have even argued that communication with the divine could only happen at a particular time. Jesus rejects all such notions. In the end, he was able to help the woman understand at least partially the truth of his words. He described to her (and to us) a new reality where God could be reached in his own world. In fact, Jesus says, he can only be reached in his dimension and that it is necessary to enter the spiritual realm to correspond with God. Simply put: God is a spiritual person and to contact him we, too, must become spiritual persons.

By putting the Eternity Principle into practice, God literally reaches from his own world into our world. This in itself is miracle enough. But there is more. It is not just that God makes contact with us and then leaves us in the same condition as we were before. On the contrary, something truly miraculous happens within us. Our spirits are brought to life by the enthusing power of the Holy Spirit. The apostle Paul makes this very clear in his letter to the Ephesians.

At the beginning of Ephesians, chapter two, Paul writes very pointedly on this spiritual transformation. The Authorized Version uses the phrase *And you hath he quickened*. That is, God awakened life where before there was no life. But, in order to make it very clear, Paul adds that we were *dead in our sins*. He draws the contrast quite starkly: We were separated from true life and were given life (quickened) by God's Spirit. This is the real power of the eternal in intimate connection with humanity. In an instant, at the moment of contact, the believer is enabled to see into the eternal realm. She becomes a truly spiritual person. And this mind-boggling event is brought about by what I am calling the Eternity Principle.

Now, the Apostle wants to leave no doubt about his message to the Ephesians. He is not satisfied to leave this matter of true spirituality here. Instead, he picks it up again in Ephesians 2:5. To make certain that he has not been misunderstood, or that some reader has missed the heart of his message, he repeats again that *we were dead in sins, [but God] brought us to life with Christ.* The contrast is unmistakable. At first we were dead. In the next moment we were alive – that is, *really alive* – for the first time.

By virtue of being created in the image of God, humans are by nature spiritual. We are indeed spiritual persons from birth. But Paul is saying that more is available. It requires the new birth for our spirits to come to life. That can only happen by the power of Christ (the same power used in creation) and it happens with the activation of the Eternity Principle.

Spirit and Connection

Christ initiated a new kind of relationship between humanity and divinity. The miracle of the Incarnation is that the Spirit of God was fused with the spirit of a human being. This was a brand new event – it had never happened before. But the ongoing miracle is that it has happened again and again since the resurrection of Christ. It is happening right now. As unbelievable as it sounds at first, the eternal Spirit of God literally melds with the spirits of humans in a continual incarnation of God's spirit.

How, then, does it happen? The major change that Christ effected was setting aside the old covenant (agreement) and instituting a new covenant. Our Bibles divide these eras into Old Testament and New Testament. The difference in the covenants – i.e., avenues of relationship between God and humanity – is the way in which we relate. Under the previous arrangement, God communicated with one person (priest, prophet, or king), who in turn spoke to all other people on God's behalf. Likewise, human beings were required to relate to God through this one person, who acted as mediator. With the recognition of Jesus as the Christ the system radically changed. Now, each person spoke directly to God for herself or himself.

During Jesus' ministry, you might say that anyone who wanted to could walk up and talk to God. That is direct access. But he realized that when he was no longer here that would not be possible. So, Jesus created a new system of spiritual connection between humanity and divinity so that direct access to God would always be available.

On the night before his crucifixion, Christ summed up the new covenant in a single phrase. In this final meeting with his disciples he revealed the possibility of ongoing communion with God by promising to send the Holy Spirit. But the miracle of this new relationship, Jesus said, was that God would not just be generally present, but literally connected with his followers. This is the simple phrase that Christ uttered which completely changed our relationship with God: *He [the Holy Spirit] dwells with you, and will be in you* (John 14:17). In one short sentence Christ inaugurated the Eternity Principle.

Suddenly our relationship with the divine takes on a new intimacy. His Spirit fuses with our spirits and we are empowered to see into the unseen realm. It would be ridiculous to suppose that the powerful force which created the universe could enter our bodies and no change take place. The Spirit actually enters into us, mingles with our spirits, brings us to life, and connects us with eternity.

Our lives, then, begin to take on real meaning. I am not saying that the lives of persons outside the Church are meaningless. But, the meaning of their lives is limited to the dimensions of space and time. Someone can build a great building, paint a great picture, or start a great movement that has no eternal implications. The Eternity Principle must be enacted within a person's life in order for her efforts in this dimension to carry over into God's dimension. If the Spirit of God is not working with the human spirit, then nothing of eternal value can take place. Certainly God could choose to use a person unaware of any divine influence, but history seems to indicate otherwise. Instead, God has chosen to work within those persons who have yielded themselves to his Spirit and who are willing for divine purposes to have precedence over human purposes.

For there to be eternal meaning to a person's life, the Eternity Principle must have been activated within that person. The Principle comes into play the moment that a person connects with God and begins to grow in influence. The Holy Spirit is at first a tiny spark within the new Christian. But the Spirit is actually present instantaneously with expressed faith (Ephesians 1:13). One does not have to wish for the Spirit to come, or hope that one day she might be worthy of the Spirit's indwelling. Quite simply, it is impossible to be a Christian without the inward presence of Christ's Spirit; likewise, one cannot be inhabited by the Spirit of Christ without being a Christian. It is illogical to suppose that an individual could somehow be a Christian and not at the same time have intimate contact with the Spirit who promises eternity.

At the absolute moment faith is expressed, then, the Holy Spirit takes up residence within the new believer. He then begins a slow, deliberate, lifetime process of perfecting the Christian (we call this sanctification). The person is no longer bound by the dimensions of space and time. He now enters eternal life and carries the hope of resurrection with Christ. In the Sermon on the Mount, Jesus promises perfection for citizens of the eternal realm. This perfection process is a vital part of the Eternity Principle. Note that Christ does not command us to be perfect. Nor does he say we will be perfected all at once. Instead, he uses the future indicative of the verb *to be* (Greek, *esesthe*), and says, in essence, *you **will be** perfect* (Matthew 5:48).

As the Eternity Principle is released in our lives, something spiritual begins to happen to us. We are made alive, as the Apostle says, and at the same time a process of perfection begins. But when we receive

Christ, receive the Spirit, and open ourselves for divine contact, our spirits are immediately brought to life, real life, and a new energy is circulated in our inner beings. This energy, or the Eternity Principle, makes us ready to move beyond the temporal into the eternal and make contact with the divine force that can create solar systems and re-create lives.

The force of creation is central to the Principle. It is in creation and re-creation that the connection is made between the physical and the spiritual. The primary reason for this is because it is the exact same force, or power, that caused the creation of the physical world that is now at work recreating believers. And the force is not sent out from God – somehow emanating from him – rather, the force actually is God. The force carries personality and identity. God's power is imprinted with God's personhood and as we relate to him, we are at the same time receiving the unseen power for life in all existing dimensions.

As persons who have made contact with divine power, we are citizens of two worlds. On the one hand, we remain trapped in space and time, fumbling through days and weeks and years. On the other hand, we move forward into agelessness, gliding through air into eternity. It is almost as if we have one foot in our own world (the realm of creation) and the other foot in God's world (the realm of re-creation). We cannot say that we are done with the present sphere of existence, but at the same time we affirm our position in the new sphere. This is what the apostle Paul means by becoming *new creatures* (2 Corinthians 5:17). A literal transformation takes place within believers and we are wonderfully changed into something brand new. We have not given up on life – we have discovered life.

ℱaith and Response

The Eternity Principle cannot function apart from faith. Absolute trust in the eternal God is prerequisite to the Principle's release. And ongoing faith is necessary to keep the Principle alive. It is not merely belief, or acceptance of factual data. It is a complete trust in the sovereign work of God in salvation and eternal life. In faith we acknowledge that God has done for us that which we were incapable of doing for ourselves. It is faith that opens the lines of communication between the human and the divine.

The faith itself is of eternal origin. It is transported from the invisible realm into the invisible human spirit. By the avenue of the Holy Spirit, the ability to believe in eternity is transferred from the mind of God to the minds of humans. This faith, once accepted, triggers the trust mechanism that has lain dormant within the spirit, and the nonbeliever is immediately recast into a believer. Simultaneously, the Eternity Principle is activated as the Spirit of God intertwines with the human spirit and the new Christian is given passage into the unseen world.

Many Christians never take advantage of their newfound freedom. Still bound by the physical dimension, they in practice ignore the reality of the spiritual dimension. Eternity is no less real, but unsure believers are unwilling to allow the invisible to function in their lives. Even though the Eternity Principle is activated in every person who turns to Christ, many of those same persons never understand the power that is now available to them. Amazingly, the ultimate creative force is just within reach, but they live as if they had no access to divine power. Rationalism completely controls these uncertain Christians and the mysterious energy of God never becomes real for them.

I am not saying that sincere believers never doubt, or that we should neglect the intellectual in favor of the affective. In fact, episodes of doubt are positive factors in the Christian's life, increasing faith once worked through. We have been made both emotional and reasonable beings and these aspects of our personhood should be balanced to achieve wholeness of identity. The danger of the 21st century is not becoming overly affective, however. The threat to spirituality in our technological age is to become overly rational – overly temporal – and to discount the reality of the unseen and the eternal.

Martin Luther, the father of the Reformation, was convinced that the inner person controlled the outer person. In other words, the mind dictates action. This is true for persons inside and outside of the Church. But the difference for the Christian is what (or better yet, Who) is controlling her mind. Jesus not only promised the indwelling of the Holy Spirit on the eve of his death, but reminded his followers that his **words** should govern their thoughts (John 15:7). Here is another important feature of the Eternity Principle: the words of Christ.

Our traditional understanding of Scripture does not rank the level of inspiration in particular passages. We hold the entire Bible as God's Word. At the same time, though, the words of Jesus carry a special authority. Not that the utterances of Old Testament prophets are any less inspired, but as the Word of God, Christ speaks the words of God in a unique way. It is vital, then, that assertions found in the Gospels have preeminence in our thinking. In the Sermon on the Mount, for example, Jesus describes in detail (often radical detail) how citizens of eternity are to live. As Christ's words become the building blocks of ethical conduct, the Eternity Principle is given a firm foundation of influence in our thinking and decision-making.

In addition, if words themselves are intrinsically substantive, then a new seriousness accompanies the use of words. There may well be a spiritual energy contained in words, which is released when words are actually spoken. This is an idea that may be difficult to grasp at first, but given some thought begins to form a logical pattern. The old adage 'sticks and stones may break my bones, but words can never harm me' may be just as false as it is catchy. If words indeed are made of something – if there is a substance or energy about them – then they can indeed affect persons and things, either harming or helping.

The Elder James insists that *the tongue* (i.e. what you say) is capable of causing irreparable destruction (James 3:5). Why? Because words themselves have a spiritual power to destroy. At the same time, however, words have power to build up and positively affect things. Isn't this what Christ means by encouraging us to store his words within our minds? By using the words of Christ, the words of faith, we can literally change situations by changing persons. Ultimately the power to change comes from our own minds and attitudes.

Just as Christ used words in all of episodes of healing (and spoke in connection with almost all of his miracles), we are able to use words to empower the Eternity Principle for our own healing. With the use of positive proclamations, I am changing the way I think, which in turn changes the way I act and react. I can literally speak my way to emotional and spiritual health. With positive words I program my brain to direct my thought-patterns. These patterns of thought, then, guide my world-view, my speech, my relationships, indeed, my world. If I continually speak negatively, thus denying the reality of eternity within me, I unplug the Eternity Principle and it is left without its vital source of power. The Principle must be united with the Holy Spirit, who infuses me with faith. And faith, as noted, is a necessary precursor of the Eternity Principle.

If I accept the fact that words are substantive, then I will be more circumspect in their use. Does this mean that a curse really has the power to destroy someone? If it is a one-time occurrence, probably not, but if I continually speak negatively toward another person, I may very well damage the person's ability to accept positive input. We know this to be true of parent-child relationships. Parents who speak affirmingly toward their children build self-esteem, confidence, and personal acceptance. Parents who downgrade their children on a regular basis hinder, perhaps even destroy, the facility for emotional well being.

For many people, because of their own histories, it is a chore to speak positively. It seems that negative thoughts and utterances come much more naturally. But, even for these people, there is a supernatural way out. When the Eternity Principle takes root in the mind, a spiritual makeover begins that will ultimately transform the individual's mode of thinking, behaving, and speaking.

It is often a very slow process with many setbacks. But with practice and a sincere desire to change, the minus speaker can be converted into a plus speaker.

Just like the initial conversion to Christianity, the conversion of words requires the power of Christ. It is the **Word**, then, who infuses us with positive, faith-filled **words**. When Christ admonishes us to speak to mountains in order to remove them from our path, he adds, *nothing is impossible* for us (Matthew 17:20). Within us, because of the activation of the Eternity Principle, we have the ability to cut through life's roadblocks with the power of words.

Often our first reaction to problems is to say *I can't*, or *it's too big*. But there is nothing too big, Jesus says. There is no possibility of impossibility in the life of faith. As we trust completely in Christ, allowing his words to control our thinking, we are capable of speaking the same words that caused the first explosion of Creation. As Christ spoke, so we can speak. His words become our words and in faith we are enthused with the creative force to demolish every spiritual obstacle, to overcome every emotional setback, to remove the mountains of hopelessness and uncertainty that threaten the activity of the Eternity Principle in our lives.

Words, then, have intrinsic energy. As the Holy Spirit inhabits our speech and rides on the air of our words, positive change begins to take place in our own lives and in the lives of those around us. I can never choose a positive attitude for another person – each individual is given the power of choice. But I can encourage those around me with the words I use. My attitude and world-view can impact my environment and those with whom I cohabitate. As I choose to live and speak positively, allowing the Eternity Principle to guide even in the choice of words, my perspective is deepened and my understanding is broadened. The substance of words can either help or hinder the work of the Spirit in my life of faith. And it is in the wisdom of Christ that I choose the words of Christ and thus animate the Eternity Principle in my mind and in my faith.

Make

a Divine

Connection

Authority and Certainty

In order for the Eternity Principle to become real for me, I must admit that something greater than me exists. I must once for all lay aside the notion that I am the center of the universe. In fact, many persons are so egocentric that they in effect act as their own god. True spirituality is either ignored or shunned and a pseudo-spirituality is set up in its place.

It is not that persons are not interested in spirituality. Humans have a natural curiosity about the invisible realm. At the same time, though, many people seem unconcerned with matters which truly pertain to God. Often we become confused about the divine and the spiritual.

God inhabits the spiritual, unseen world. But we must remember that our spirits are brought to life by his Spirit in order to contact the invisible realm. In the final analysis, God initiates contact and there is no way to enter the unseen apart from his Spirit. So, we must be careful to truly make a divine connection.

If I set up myself as life's ultimate authority, then I am denying the testimony of the physical dimension. Creation shouts **There is a God!** by its order, design, and structure. The universe itself is evidence that a thinking, powerful being (God) exists and exerted his creative force to bring it into reality. If the whole of Creation, which is greater than me, testifies to the purposes of God, how can I then claim to hold ultimate authority separately? Instead, I must submit to the greater authority and look to him for truth, life, and indeed, being.

Scripture, then, plays an extremely important role in revealing the truths of this ultimate authority. In short, the Bible shows us who God is. By relinquishing the right to be an authority unto myself, I come to understand real authority. Scripture contains all of the principles necessary for the life of faith, and it has within it the principles of eternity. Just as faith and eternity go hand-in-hand, so the Bible and the Eternity Principle work together to reveal Christ in the spirit of the believer.

Interestingly, ultimate authority comes from without and within. Authority is explained in Scripture and moves through the Holy Spirit. In other words, rule originates with God (from without) and is transported to us in Spirit and in Word. Yet, once here, authority is activated (within us) by the Eternity Principle. The Spirit brings us to life, mobilizes the Eternity Principle, and in effect transfers the unseen authority into our invisible beings. It is a continual loop whereby the Spirit maintains the connection between human and divine, always giving preference to the divine will. As we in turn give that same preference, releasing to the divine our own wills in subjection to the authority of Christ, we acknowledge the greater rule, remove egocentrism, and unleash the eternal power of God into our lives.

While our link to the divine is not based solely on Scripture, it is nonetheless foundational to our relationship with God. The words of Scripture reflect the special divine-human interaction that we come to know through the Eternity Principle. Each proclaimer, or writer endowed Scripture with his own understanding of the divine and his own experience of eternity. God has always chosen to accomplish his purposes in the dimension of space and time through human agency. The same is true of Scripture. The divine joined the human in spiritual proclamation, which has drawn persons in all ages to relationship with eternity.

Yet, we must remember that our knowledge of God is not grounded in Scripture alone. We know of him through the traditions of the Church. We know of him in our relationships with other believers. We know of him because of the indwelling of his Spirit. To be sure, the subjective of tradition and relationship can never supersede the objective of the written Word. But the very real testimonies of faithful people across the ages are invaluable. The Spirit is alive within us and opens our eyes to the truths of Scripture. Just as our spirits are eternally intertwined with the Spirit of God, so the objective witness and the subjective testimony are continually cooperating to reveal to us a more complete picture of the eternal and the unseen.

For Christians, the Bible must finally be the ultimate authority for ethical and moral conduct. In it we find spiritual principles for living out faith. Throughout its pages we come to know of other saints in other times who grappled with the unseen world in the same way as we saints in this time. Scripture shows us who we are to be, it teaches us our spiritual vocabulary, and it lays down the ground rules for becoming a citizen of eternity. Its preservation through the centuries is proof enough of its divine affinity and in faith we accept its objective truths as counsel for living.

Principle and Promise

The Eternity Principle remains for us the promise of divine activity within. By its activation, the Holy Spirit awakens our spirits and connects us with divine energy. It is by this principle that we are empowered to see into the unseen; to touch the invisible; to experience eternity.

Though the term is absent from Scripture, its connotation is present on each page and between every line. This principle is the power of God himself within us, enabling us to communicate with the invisible. By its laws we traverse the dimensions of time and eternity. But we must be careful to always realize that the principle is inextricably linked to personality. It is God's personal Spirit who energizes our personal spirits. The principle is validated through the direct, ongoing union of humanity and divinity.

The dimensional elements are truly exciting. When we come to understand the Eternity Principle, we also accept the nearness of the unseen world. The spiritual realm is not far away, but is indeed very close. We experience God in our dimension, as well as his, and we know him both in this life and in the one yet to be.

Summary

**God works in us through
the Eternity Principle**

**The Eternity Principle
is activated and appropriated
personally**

**We are empowered
to spiritually enter eternity**

**Faith enables
the Eternity Principle
to be released in our lives**

**Scripture and the Holy Spirit
are the sure authority
for our lives as spiritual persons**

Miracles Happen Within Us

We have searched into the depths of divine knowledge

~ Clement of Rome ~

Book Two
Within and Beyond

The Eternal Perspective

Where do you begin? In each of us there is the innate desire to touch the spiritual, but the question inevitably comes: Where do I begin? The place to begin is what I call the **Eternity Principle**. With it we can start our search for God and his kingdom.

First, how do we personalize spirituality? A mystic searches within the soul to find the divine spark that can infuse life's power into everyday existence. The idea is that the only reason you haven't yet discovered the unseen power available to you is because you have not reached deep enough inside yourself. You, by virtue of your humanity and connection with cosmic reality, can and will find the ultimate power within yourself: because that is where ultimate reality exists, inside of you.

A strict transcendentalist would argue that it is completely outside of yourself that reality is found. You have become trapped in a human body, but that is not the real you. On the contrary, the way to touch the spiritual, and indeed the way to discover life's power, is to completely divorce your consciousness from the physical realm – to project your mind out of yourself – so that you can contact the invisible and the spiritual.

Since all purity (indeed, holiness) is to be found outside of personality, the quicker you exclude personhood from your thinking, the quicker you will touch the divine.

What of the biblical perspective? Is mysticism right to look within? Yes. But with this qualifier: What is it (or better yet *Who* is it) that you find when you look within yourself? A central part of the radical change that Christ made in the new covenant was the concept of an indwelling Holy Spirit. Remember what Jesus said: "you know him because he is *with* you, and will be *inside of* you" (John 14:17, my emphasis). For the Christian, then, the divine actually, literally abides (resides, lives) within. The apostle Paul is clear when he says that at the instant of conversion, the believer is sealed with the Holy Spirit (Ephesians 1:13). What then? Simply this: We are able to look within to touch the spiritual because the Spirit himself is inside of us.

In the same way, a transcendentalist is correct when she insists that we get outside of ourselves. Is all of God contained within individual Christians? In the Church? We would shout a resounding No! God is the Other. He is holy and unlike human beings, except in his voluntary incarnation and identification with us through subsuming human nature. This does not impute his holiness, however, but only makes his purity more real to us in the vivid images of a man who could live among us and yet not accept death like the rest. The transcendentalist is right: We must get out of ourselves – reach beyond our human natures – in order to touch the spiritual. But we must not make the mistake of impugning personality or disdaining the physical. The message of scripture is clear: God is a person, who made human persons in his image. At the same time, God created the physical universe and deemed it "good" (Genesis 1). We are not to reject that which God has deemed good. We connect with the divine through personal relationship and live our lives (here and in the resurrection) in bodies.

So, the testimony of the Bible is this: We touch the spiritual within ourselves and beyond ourselves. It is both/and. Now the question becomes: Why should I begin with the Bible? Simple: no other book of religion offers a personal relationship with God. It is a relationship that he offers to us freely. Other books show a powerful God; a God of justice; a God to be worshipped; but only the Bible shows a God who wants to know you. Personally. Up close. Eye-to-eye. This is the God the Bible presents.

And that is the God that I present in this book. He is the One you can find through the Eternity Principle. And you will find him Within and Beyond.

Person and Practice

How can someone expect to de-personalize spirituality? As humans, we are personality. There is no way around it. We know ourselves and other human beings as persons. It is in relationship that we are able to develop and become the persons that we want to be. How, then, do we expect to experience the spiritual, or the divine, apart from person-to-person contact? Since I cannot know myself apart from personhood – and indeed know of no other way to experience reality – it is absurd to imagine that I can discover the unseen, spiritual realm in some non-personal way. On every page of scripture the truth of personhood is made clear. God, a person, created us as persons and it is in relationship with him that we can see into the unseen.

Do I look within? Yes. Do I look beyond? Yes. But I must look through the spectacles of ego and personality into the eyes and mind of another person to truly contact the spiritual nature that I continually long to touch.

One of the keys to Christianity is balance. "Moderation in all things," said Socrates, and the New Testament writers put this theme in religious language. So, whether we are talking about eating or drinking or work or play, we approach all of life in moderation. Christianity is a balanced religion. While this is readily seen in the practice of the religion in our everyday lives, it is not always so apparent when it comes to spirituality. But that is, in fact, where it begins. It is the inner/outer balance of our spirituality that is the foundation for the balance and moderation in our practice.

But how do we get there? Can we just suddenly become spiritual? Not exactly. To be sure, a person is born spiritually at the moment she decides to become a Christian. She does not have to mail in an application form for spiritual awakening. It begins immediately. At the same time, though, we must recognize that it has only begun. It is not finished at the instant it starts. Rather a process begins so that the new Christian is increasingly aware of her spiritual nature. Someone has said that *a person is as spiritual as he or she chooses to be*. A freewill choice is at the heart of personal spirituality.

It is just like a student being placed in a classroom. The teacher is there, other students are there, information is being shared, learning is going on, but the student may or may not choose to participate. We cannot force someone to learn. We may be able to put him in an environment where learning is possible. We may even equip him with all the necessary tools for learning. But the student will learn only if he chooses to take advantage of the opportunity given to him.

The same is true in personal spirituality. A person is only as spiritual as she chooses to be. Or maybe, as she chooses to *become*. Spirituality is an evolving, progressive unveiling of the person within. It is the enlightening of the mind and slowly we are brought to full consciousness by the inner work of God's Spirit. But each of us holds the key to our own spirituality. I can choose to become a spiritual person, or I can turn away from the opportunity given to me and regress to the starting point.

It's really all up to me. And all up to you. You can become the person God created you to be, but first you must choose to become that person. It is not automatic. God will not force you to mature and accept the new responsibilities he has planned for you. On the contrary, he will only present the possibilities, and even then the choices are not always clear cut. You must search for God and allow his Spirit to enliven your spirit to the point that you can begin to see all the opportunities available. God does not reveal himself in a haphazard way. Instead, after he has called you, he will wait for you to seek him.

St. Augustine said:

I look for God in the material effects of heaven and earth, but I have not found him. I [also] look for the reality of God in my own soul, but I have not found his reality. Still, I am determined to search for my God.

Augustine diligently looked for God, but soon discovered that divine consciousness was not to be found at every turn. He looked for him in both the temporal and eternal realms. He desperately searched for God within his own mind and spirit. God was there. He is always there. Still Augustine could not quite touch him. God was just out of reach. But Augustine passionately wanted to become a spiritual person. "I am determined to search for my God," he said. Nothing was going to deter him from finding God and uncovering the spiritual nature that God had placed within him.

Freewill, choice, and determination are requisite to fully discovering God and completely understanding our-selves. Perseverance is necessary if we truly want to become spiritual. We are only as spiritual as we choose to be and the choosing can only come from within each of us. I cannot choose for you and you cannot choose for me. You will become spiritually aware by exercising your freewill and determining that you will indeed touch eternity.

The Eternity Principle makes it clear. The spiritual realm is within reach, but we must look both within and beyond ourselves in order to fully comprehend the unseen world. It exists within you and it is a reality outside of you. Until you understand this inner/outer duality of eternity, and see its perfect balance as both an idea and a concrete reality, you will be unable to appreciate all that the invisible world has to offer.

Attributes and Aspirations

It is impossible to quantify eternity. Still, it is helpful to attempt to get some kind of grasp on how eternity is structured. Christ depicted eternity as a kingdom – an actual place – where we could live and exercise our rights as citizens. It is indeed a place, but it is also an idea, a dream, a hope. Eternity is both within us and beyond us and must be captured by our minds and our aspirations at the same time.

While admitting that eternity cannot be fully explained or understood, we still want to understand as much about the unseen world as we possibly can. The attributes of eternity are innumerable, for with such things as timelessness, boundlessness, and total abundance, how can we expect to add up all the features we find in Christ's kingdom? However, I believe there are three foundational elements, or attributes, to eternity. These three attributes form the bedrock of the kingdom upon which everything else is built.

The three foundational attributes of eternity are *Life, Agape (Love), and the Mind of Christ.*

Life. The most powerful force in the universe is life.

Nothing can overwhelm it. Life always comes out on top. In view of eternity, even death has to finally give way to the pervasiveness and persistence of life. Certainly death may for a moment seem to be victorious, but when real life is involved, death itself is annihilated as the flow of life again rushes through to restart consciousness and re-spark the will and the power to live.

The Gospel of John is explicit: "In him was life, and this life was really the light of humanity" (1:4). Christ possesses life and has the authority and power to give it to us. Life actually resides within the person of Christ. "In him was life," John writes. Life is inside of Christ, energizing his being, emanating from him, empowering his mind, strengthening his will, and enlightening his consciousness. The same force that caused the initial explosion of the Big Bang is resident in Christ. He holds the ultimate power of the universe and he offers this power to you and to me.

According to John, Christ and God are one and the same person (1:1). When we think of an intelligent being actively involved in creation, we can go beyond some faceless and nameless god. Jesus Christ was present in the beginning, was active in the creative process of designing the universe, and was responsible for releasing the awesome power necessary to propel the universe into existence (John 1:2-3). He still possesses this power and, in fact, is still responsible for the molecular cohesion of the universe, because he still possesses the power of life which causes our world to continue to exist.

But there is something more to this life than just raw power. John says that it is because of our conscious connection with Christ that we are enlightened. "This life is the light of humanity," he writes (1:4). So, Christ not only gives us the power to be alive, but he also gives us the power to become conscious. Our conscious awareness separates human beings from lower life forms. We have the freedom to connect with divinity and become aware of our world, who we are, and how we relate to our environment. Every human being is given this light, or consciousness. You do not have to be a person of faith in order to enjoy the privilege of the enlightenment offered by Christ. You are self-aware simply because you are human.

Note, though, that there is a qualitative and quantitative difference between life and eternal life. Believers and non-believers alike are alive on planet earth and going about their various day-to-day activities. They are, in short, all alive. And what is more, they are all enlightened. But that is where the similarity ends and an all important difference begins. Because of the Eternity Principle, persons of faith have the promise of ongoing, never-ending life. The life of a believer is eternal. The life of each normal human being will one day cease. The person will die and that will be the end of it. In the case of the non-believer, death really does have the final say. Life is exterminated by death. But this is not the case with the believer, because she has connected with the source of life. She has chosen to relate to Christ one-on-one and the power and the freedom to live have been granted to her by divine decree. She has accepted the truth of the Eternity Principle and it in turn gives her the power of eternal life.

So there is an enhanced enlightenment, or consciousness, for the person of faith. This is what Jesus means when he says that the Eternity Principle actually enables an individual to see into his invisible kingdom (John 3:3). The believer has a heightened, more sensitive, awareness of reality. He knows something more about the make-up of the world than the average person. His eyes have been opened and he is able to see into eternity and to understand how the eternal, unseen realm can affect life in his own world.

The Eternity Principle, then, cannot operate apart from the power of life. Christ made it clear that if we are disconnected from his power, we are unable to affect our circumstances with any real consequence (John 15:5). It is his power working in us and through us that empowers us. Christ's power is both an internal and external force, but it always begins in the unseen. His kingdom functions in the invisible realm and so connects with us in our unseen, inner selves. His life must first be at work in us before it can influence our environment. That is simply the order of things, from the unseen to the seen, from the idea to the product. Life is active within us, enthusing us, and we in turn are able to cause things to happen around us.

As one of eternity's foundational attributes, Life is the conduit through which Christ's invisible power flows from his kingdom into our lives. Further, without Life, not only would our existence come to an end, but eternity could not continue either. To say that there could be eternity without Life is like saying there could be life on earth as we know it without an atmosphere. It is simply impossible. Life is the energy which drives eternity ever forward, always keeping eternity in motion. Christ's kingdom is not at a standstill. It is forever moving forward, forever becoming something new. Life always recreates everything around it into something new and better.

Just as the Eternity Principle itself works within us and beyond us, so, too, Life works in the same way. The attribute of Life is inside of us, energizing our spirits, and igniting within us a kind of spiritual atomic explosion that radiates throughout our entire beings. And as the power of Life grows within us, we are soon empowered to reach beyond us to help others find real Life. Like the other two eternal attributes, it is not an isolated characteristic of eternity. Instead, Life permeates the entire unseen realm, infusing it with an irrepressible vitality that energizes both the invisible kingdom and its citizens. Life cannot be suppressed and its nature makes it more than an attribute. It is, after all, *Life*.

Agape. The second foundational attribute of eternity is Agape, or selfless Love. Love not only makes the world go around, but it also allows eternity to operate. Love is the natural companion of Life. Whenever real, eternal Life is present, Love is always there, too. Since Life is a pure, holy force, infusing everything around it with invisible energy, it carries with it all that is holy and pure. And Agape, self-sacrificing Love, is the most holy attribute in existence.

The everyday Greek language of the first century CE (the one used to write the New Testament) was very expressive. Often there was more than one word to describe a particular virtue, so that the reader or hearer would understand exactly what the writer or speaker was communicating. This is the case with the word 'love.'

The Greeks actually had four words to depict four different kinds of love. Everything from friendship to romantic love is expressed through these words. But Agape, or selfless Love, is the highest, most complete form of love. (For an excellent exposition of this subject, see C.S. Lewis, *The Four Loves).*

Ultimately, we must connect with divinity in order to experience this pinnacle of love, Agape. In its most pure form, only God possesses Agape. But the exciting news is that he is willing to share it with us. Basic to the whole notion of Agape, self-sacrificing Love, is that the person who has it has an irresistible desire to give this Love to others. When Agape takes over, you actually can't *not* give it away.

The Eternity Principle itself is based on Agape. "For God so loved (agape) the world," the Bible says, "that he gave to the world his only son; and anyone and everyone who trusts completely in him will receive eternal life" (John 3:16). God's love for us caused him to exercise his self-sacrificing Love and give his only son as a means of our reaching into eternity and touching the divine. In other words, God sent his son from the eternal realm into our realm, thus once and forever connecting the two spheres and allowing free passage back and forth from our world into God's world. And Agape is the power of that connection and the force that allows safe passage into the divine, eternal realm.

Agape, though, is more than a power; it is more than

a conduit for contacting eternity. Agape is one of the foundation stones of eternity. Without Agape God's eternal realm could not exist. Just as there could be no life without the supreme source of life, so, too, there could be no holiness and purity and compassion without their source. That source is Love. It is Agape that saturates eternity so that the realm is substantive and able to remain intact. It is Agape that undergirds the attributes of Life and holiness, so that they are able to give power to eternity and its citizens. Agape is the substance, the stuff, of eternity and if it were suddenly removed, the Eternity Principle would be unplugged and eternity itself would be unable to hold together.

So, then, how does it work? How does Agape retain its power to accomplish its very necessary task? The Bible puts it simply: "God is Love" (1 John 4:8). In other words, just as the other two foundational attributes, Love has a personal quality. God and Agape are intimately related; they are, in fact, the same entity. The supreme resident of eternity and self-sacrificing Love are one and the same and they cannot be separated. God has made this kind of Love available to us through the Eternity Principle. This means, in fact, that he has made himself available to us.

This section from John's first letter bears more scrutiny. Here, he shows the intrinsic relationship between Agape and the Eternity Principle. "Everyone who expresses Love has been brought to life by God and knows God," John writes. "If anyone does not express [real] Love, he does not actually know who God is, because God is Love" (1 John 4:7-8). The author is saying that when the Eternity Principle is activated ("brought to life by God"), Love is the natural result. The Eternity Principle cannot operate apart from Love, just as eternity itself cannot do so. But when a person connects with eternity, and spiritual power is released in her life, one of the foundational attributes that she will find herself in possession of is Agape. By relating to God through Christ, the new believer touches and receives not only God himself, but the eternal attributes as well. When I touch God, I touch Love and a brand new kind of compassion and empathy is born within me and I see other people through different eyes. The eyes of eternity.

When I am given Agape through the Eternity Principle, then I actually "know God" (1 John 4:7). Conversely, if I have not discovered what Love is, then I cannot at the same time claim to know something about divine nature. Love and God are the same and to know and experience the one is to have intimate knowledge of the other.

When God chose to "love the world" (John 3:16), he reached out from his eternal world into our temporal realm. But the very act of reaching out caused our own world to become permeated by the attributes of God.

Now, by virtue of the Eternity Principle, we can choose to relate to God and discover the real meaning of selfless Love. Agape, although originating in eternity, can be effectively used in our own world by eternal persons who know God.

Mind of Christ. The third, and final, foundational attribute of eternity is the Mind of Christ. The creation of the universe was first imagined in the divine mind before it became an objective, physical reality. The idea always precedes the product. Socrates insists that a proper system of thought leads to a proper mode of action. In other words, the kinds of things we think about will ultimately manifest themselves in our words, actions, and relationships. Christ first envisioned a galaxy and then created the Milky Way. He first imagined a loving relationship and then created human beings to love. The idea comes first and then is followed by an action. If it is a good idea, then good, proper actions will follow. But the reverse is true, as well, which reminds us of the importance of maintaining positive, loving, creative thoughts.

In his letter to the Philippians (4:8), Paul draws the picture very clearly:

Finally, my brothers, discover the things that are true and admirable; the things that are right and virtuous; the things that are beautiful and commendable; the things that are exceptional and worthy of celebration, and then keep your minds and thoughts focused on them.

Paul understands that action proceeds from thought. He admonishes us to keep our minds filled with good thoughts, with pure images, so that our actions toward other people will be ethical and moral and right. When we fill our minds with these positive ideas, Paul says, God's peace permeates every part of our beings and brings us ever closer to eternity (Philippians 4:9).

But, how do we locate these wonderful thoughts to begin with? How can we transform our thinking from negative, depressing, lifeless patterns into positive, uplifting, life-giving patterns? In short, how do I leave my old thinking behind and begin to think the thoughts of eternity? Again, Paul is clear when he says that believers are in possession of *the Mind of Christ* (1 Corinthians 2:16). When a person comes into contact with Christ, and the Eternity Principle is activated, her mind is immediately connected by spiritual energy with God's mind. She is able to tap into God's thought-patterns and change her thought-process from negative to positive. Through the Eternity Principle the new believer takes on the Mind of Christ.

The Apostle John, in his Gospel, leaves nothing to

question. It was through the creativity of Christ's mind that the entire universe came into being (1:1-4). Christ (The Word) imagined vast expanses of space filled with stars and planets, with light and darkness, with solar systems and galaxies. And he thought of people on the planet Earth (and elsewhere?) and he visualized those people in relationship with him and with one another. Christ imagined all of these things *first*. And then he created them. Thought precedes action and Christ possesses all thought, all creativity, and all imagination. He pictured a world and that world came into existence at the performance of his will. The Mind of Christ, then, is the ultimate source of life and creation.

And believers have that mind. To be a 'Christian' is to be like Christ. How could we possibly be like him without thinking like him? We have the power, because of the Eternity Principle, to tap into the thoughts of God and to make those thoughts our own. And once those pure and holy thoughts become ours, pure and holy actions will be the natural outcome. There is no barrier between the believer and eternity, and the essence of eternity is Christ's thoughts – his Mind.

You are as spiritual as you choose to be. You can choose the Mind and the thoughts and the creativity of Christ at any time. The Eternity Principle is real and it really works. At any point in time you can choose to connect with God, allow his spirit to enliven your spirit, and begin using the Mind of Christ to map out a perfect plan for your life.

In the human body, the brain is the command center of all activity. If there is a glitch in the neurological system and messages from the brain do not reach, say, your right hand, then your right hand will remain motionless. It will be unable to perform any task. The brain sends pulses of energy throughout the body, commanding specific actions.

It is the same with the eternal brain: the Mind of Christ. His energetic thoughts pulsate throughout the universe to cause forces of gravity to hold, comets to stay on track, and human beings to love one another. Christ's mind is the command center of physical and spiritual activity and we can, if we choose, adopt his thoughts as our own and face life with a powerful arsenal of creativity and inspiration.

The Mind of Christ undergirds creation itself. Unless the universe had first been conceived in his Mind, it could not have become a reality within time and space. The ideas came first and then the products followed. But his creativity was not a one-time burst of energy. It is not as if Christ used up all of his ideas in producing the world as it now exists. That was only the beginning. His Mind is the source of ongoing, life-producing, ever-creative patterns of thought that empower us with universal ideas to confront universal challenges.

These foundational attributes of Life, Love, and Mind fuse into a unified force that enables the universe, and us, to function. Life is the constantly evolving source of all that exists, which is expressed through the process of thought and Mind. And Agape, self-sacrificing Love is the energy which drives life forward and makes the Eternity Principle not only powerful, but personal.

So, we find God within ourselves and beyond ourselves. He is quite near and he is transcendent all at the same time. What is clear is that we cannot focus only on the inner or outer experience of eternity, while ignoring the other very real reality. Instead, we must find ways to join the inner experience of spirituality with the outer experience of religion and service. It is both within and beyond that you will discover God. And both places must be explored with the same intensity and devotion.

Seen and Unseen

How do we come into contact with God? This chasm between the seen and the unseen often seems impossible to cross. We are aware of God in the seen: The universe around us testifies to his presence. There is the order and design of creation ever present which solemnly, continually tell that God was and is here. Just now thunder is clapping loudly outside my window. It seems with every peal to be the voice of God saying *I Am Here*.

Through faith we accept the presence of God. Sometimes we personalize this concept to the point of forgetting his omnipresence. We know that God is with us, but we sometimes forget that he is in all places at all times. Perhaps this thought is too big for us. This is where the chasm between seen and unseen becomes too wide for our imaginations. We can sense that God is with us, but how can he at the same time be with others on another continent? C. S. Lewis in *Beyond Personality* (1944) gives one of the better analogies of how this might work. He likens God to a novelist who is writing about a particular character in a particular scene. Although the novelist could leave the scene in the middle of a paragraph and not return for hours or days, no time has elapsed for the fictional character. In the same way, God, operating above time, is able to interact with individual persons in their own time. There is a yearning inside of us for divine contact with God. As persons of faith we think of the divine and human intermingling in the person of Christ and our imaginations soar. How did he feel? What was it like for the man Jesus to be in living, breathing contact with the eternal God? In one man, in a moment in time, the finite and the infinite converged, melded, and in that moment eternity touched the sundial and changed history.

These thoughts thrill us and as long as we speak only of divine/human contact in the person of Christ we are comfortable in the conversation. But, then, the discussion begins to include us. How can we as humans contact the divine? How can the seen and the unseen again converge within the confines of time?

Christ prayed that the oneness he experienced with God might also connect us with the divine and create a new kind of unity here on earth (John 17). Christ reveals the unseen to us. He cracks the door between the dimensions of time and eternity and allows us to peek through to the other side. In Christ the seen and the unseen are joined and through him we are empowered to experience that which would otherwise be forbidden to us.

We contact God through personal relationship with

Christ. God is attainable: he has made himself so for our sakes. The invisible became visible so that we might see our way to salvation. The Bible leads to salvation and in that sense reveals God. But the scriptures only reveal the things of God that he has chosen to reveal. He is still the unseen. He still inhabits eternity. He is still wrapped in mystery. The Apostle Paul says "at present we cannot focus clearly on eternity" (1 Corinthians 13:12). There is still much unseen about God. In eternity itself we will see God clearly, completely, and wonderfully as he is.

So, to contact God, I must allow the unseen to become real to me. I must admit that there is much I do not know. I must come to know the Christ of the gospel, as best as I can, because in him the unseen is seen. And I must let God reveal himself to me in his own time, so that his reality begins to become the reality in which I live. In this way, the unseen God touches the unseen me and the invisible parts of me slowly manifest themselves into the visible world in which I move. Contact is made with God, and suddenly, I am able to see more than I ever before imagined.

In a very real sense, in order to know Christ, I must first know myself.

But how do I see the unseen within myself? How can I come to know who I truly am? Curiously enough, we come to know ourselves by a deepening understanding of God; and we come to know God by a deepening understanding of ourselves. I cannot know God without knowing me; and I cannot know myself without knowing God. Which comes first? Both. While I am seeking God (outwardly), I am seeking me (inwardly). And as the Holy Spirit resides in me, I am contacting God here as well. Internally and externally I find God and little by little the unseen within me is revealed.

As the Eternity Principle is released within me, my mind is fused to the Mind of Christ. As the Principle grows within me, and as I continue to seek God, the Mind of Christ slowly takes over. The thinking and the ideas of God become mine. Through the Eternity Principle I can actually tap into the unsearchable mind of God and retrieve his creativity, his wisdom, his intuitiveness. And by searching the unknowable Mind of Christ, I somehow illuminate the unseen me.

The more we know about ourselves, the more we will know about God. If we know how our minds work, how our thought-processes move us to do certain things, how our cognitive development interplays with our moral and social development, then we come nearer to understanding divine thought-processes. Mind is connected to mind and by knowing ourselves, we know God.

The Eternity Principle must be enacted for a person to

come into full contact with God. Once eternity touches the human mind, that mind is brought to full life. It is brought, in effect, online. It is reprogrammed with divine thinking and the new believer is able to begin the process of rewriting, or reformatting, her mind so that divine thoughts begin to supersede human thoughts.

Mind and Thought

There is, of course, nothing wrong with human thoughts. They are, after all, given by God. But there is a qualitative and quantitative difference between the human mind and the Mind of Christ. My mind is limited; his is unlimited. I can become confused; he is never confused. I have almost certain probability of forgetting information; Christ never forgets anything (except what he *chooses* to forget). In short, Christ possesses a perfect mind and I do not.

But there remains the promise, "You will be perfect in the same way that God is perfect" (Matthew 5:48). The perfection of our minds begins when the Eternity Principle is released within us and allowed to start its work. Our human minds are tuned-up by the perfect, complete mind of Christ.

This desire to have the Mind of Christ is ongoing for the believer. As I continue to learn about myself, and my own knowledge and psyche grow, I will have the capacity, and the desire, to learn more about God. It is impossible to know all about myself in one moment, and it is even more impossible to know God in one moment (or one trillion moments). In fact, I will never completely know God. He is unsearchable and unknowable. God is unchanging, yet he is always new.

God's purpose has not changed. His character has not changed. At the same time, though, God is forever new to us. To use a simple analogy: A rose bush puts out beautiful red roses every year. Each year it is the same red roses. But, are they the *same* roses? No, the red roses this year are new roses. They are still roses, they are still beautiful, they still have a sweet aroma, but they are not the very same roses that came forth last year. But they did come from the same source, the same root, the same bush. They are the same, yet they have changed.

This is how it is with God. The Love that he expressed to believers centuries ago is not the same Love he is expressing to you. The Life that he activated in Abraham and Moses is not the same Life that he has activated in you. It is new Life. It is forever new. But its source is the same. The Eternity Principle springs from the same God, but it is always fresh and always a new experience for each new believer.

This brings up the interesting phrase from the first chapter of the Gospel of John, "in him was Life" (1:4). John goes to some trouble to explain to us that Christ was connected with creation. He insists, in fact, that no part of creation would exist apart from the activity of "the Word" (Greek, *logos*, i.e. divine reason, creative force). He then connects this *Word* with the person Christ (John 1:14). For the Apostle John, then, Christ was present and active at the creation of the universe.

By way of describing this activity, John puts forth the idea "in him was Life." In this short phrase is a universe of meaning. First of all, notice that John says "in him." For emphasis, read it this way: IN him. John is pointing to the unseen nature of God. There was something inside of this Word, he seems to be saying, that we would be unable to detect with our senses. It was inner, intrinsic. But it was most definitely there. The unseen, invisible character of a particular quality does not diminish its reality. It may have been unseen, John would maintain, but it was nonetheless present and real.

But what was this unseen quality? "In him was Life," the Gospel reads. Again for emphasis, read the phrase: IN him was LIFE. In four words John connects the unseen reality with a particular quality. He is contending for the presence of Life itself within the divine Word. Within the person of Christ, Life exists, resides, finds meaning, and is given its source of power. And Life is never static. Life is not changeless. Life is alive. It is moving, evolving, changing, becoming. Life does not sit still, but is constantly, continuously on the move. Life changes directions. Life becomes more alive in the next moment than it was in the moment before, because if it did not it would not be Life. It would be death.

But the Gospel is clear. It is not death that is resident in Christ. It is Life. The person of Jesus Christ is not a static icon. Instead he represents the most alive human that has ever entered the pages of history. Since he is *logos* (divine), but at the same time human, the connection of unseen divinity with seen humanity is coupled with such life-giving power that neither the invisible nor the visible is reduced. To be sure, Life was *in* him. But Life has such universal power that it cannot be contained. It may begin as unseen, but soon enough Life breaks through to be experienced. Its power cannot be curtailed and in the end the alive, powerful, all-consuming Life overwhelms everything that surrounds it.

This is why death cannot be resident in Christ. He is so full of Life that it drives out death once and for all. "Death has been destroyed," the Apostle Paul writes (1 Corinthians 15:54). Death has been obliterated. It has been overwhelmed by the more powerful force of Life and it simply falls before its greater sibling. *In him was Life* and that Life, because of its very nature, is an ongoing, continuous reality.

This is why it is impossible to speak of Christ in the past tense. Even John, when he writes "in him *was* Life" (to underscore the presence of Christ at creation), cannot keep up the pretense of the past. This Life was the very light of humanity, he says (John 1:4), but this is the light that *shines* (present tense) in the darkness (John 1:5). Christ is alive now and the Life within him continues its creative force. The darkness cannot remain true to its nature when light is introduced. *Un-life* cannot exist in the presence of Life. And the past becomes dim when compared to an alive present. We cannot speak of God as a 'has-been.' God is. And the Life which was once unseen became astoundingly visible when Christ chose to reveal it.

At first, then, Life was present (although unseen) in Christ. It was within him eagerly seeking release. God is, of course, totally self-aware and had a full sense of Life's activity within. At the moment of the creation (the Big Bang), God chose to release Life and to reveal himself to the universe. He knows who he is and the only way that we know him is because he has chosen to reveal himself to us. In the same way, we are empowered to know ourselves, because God releases this same Life within our spirits. The Eternity Principle is engaged and we begin to know ourselves and our world.

This process of a gradual self-awareness is what we learn about in the Garden Story in the first three chapters of Genesis. Humans slowly became aware of their environment, of God, of themselves. It did not happen all at once. There was an evolutionary process by which humanity became conscious, self-aware. This is what the story of the Garden tells us. The Eternity Principle was in place from the very beginning, but it was introduced by process.

The Eternity Principle slowly but surely made an inroad into the human mind. Identity emerged and humans realized their own reality. And, ultimately, they came to know the reality of God.

Karl Barth, the gifted German theologian, believed that in order to connect with God, a person must be self-involved. In other words, even though God is reaching out from eternity, hoping to contact an individual, the connection cannot happen as long as the person is passive. Each of us must take action in order to come to know God. The divine-human connection requires that both the divine person and the human person are actively seeking the other.

Here again we see what makes the Eternity Principle so exciting. In order for the Principle to be activated, I must take action to turn it on. Eternity won't just happen to me. To be sure, God is lovingly searching for me, urging me to become one with him. But I can refuse the connection. I can turn away. My freewill is intact and I have the choice of going my own way. I must choose the Eternity Principle in order for it to be real for me.

Freedom and Salvation

The Eternity Principle is exciting because it is voluntary. I don't have to accept it. I can choose to live my life apart from a relationship with God. But what kind of life? The New Testament is clear: Life without Christ is no life at all. In fact, it is walking death. But by freely choosing to activate the Eternity Principle, the unseen becomes real in my life and in fact is no longer unseen. It can be seen by me; it can be seen by those around me. "I don't know what happened," someone will say, "but you sure are different now." The unseen has become visible and even other people will be able to see the activity of the Eternity Principle.

In order for salvation to be complete, I must choose to turn on the Eternity Principle day after day in my life. The Holy Spirit takes control of my spirit, I am brought to life again and again, and eventually I come to resemble Christ. So salvation is a process whereby I slowly evolve in my identification with the divine. It is a process that will never end as I spend eternity becoming more and more like God, resembling him more and more, becoming more and more faithful.

In the end seen and unseen become the same. The Eternity Principle makes God so real for you that you are eventually able to see him in your actions; hear him in your words; recognize him in your thoughts.

In Jesus the seen and the unseen became one. Christ embodied both the visible and the invisible. Is the unseen within you, as well? Absolutely.

Getting to know yourself, however, is a tough job. Mainly because there is so little that you actually can know. But even the parts that you can know, when touched, can be quite painful. It seems that everyone has some sort of hurt in the past. You may not have been physically abused, but the psychology of families is so strange sometimes, that it is virtually impossible to grow up without some scars.

Are we willing to face that past pain? Because if we have not faced it, it is in fact not in the past, but is a pain that still haunts. Will we confront the pains of misunderstanding, of hurt, of emotional neglect or abuse? If we are unwilling to face these issues in our lives, then we can never truly know ourselves, and in turn cannot know God. These pains are unseen and we want to keep them that way. To come into our own identities, however, they must be uncovered, exposed for what they really are, and finally and completely banished from our consciousness. And this is possible by using the Eternity

Principle.

It is a paradox: As we come to know God more, we better understand ourselves; and as we come to terms with who we really are, we come to know more of God. As we reach into the unseen within ourselves, we are at the same time touching the unseen God, because he is there too. The Eternity Principle has been activated, the Holy Spirit resides within, and when the invisible parts of us are discovered, so too the unseen God becomes manifest within us.

But dealing with the pain is not easy. It is not quickly resolved. Again, Christ guides us through the pain, shines his light on it, reveals it for what it really is, and we come out on the other side more Christ-like than we were before. It was by identifying with our suffering that Christ became most like us. And it is by entering into our suffering with him that we become more like him.

And here another paradox emerges: We are healed by going through the pain, not by avoiding it. We can never really avoid pain. We only trick ourselves into believing that we can. It is still there. It is eating away at our consciousness and our spirituality. It actually becomes bigger than we are and threatens to overwhelm us, but there is a way out. As we make the Eternity Principle real in our lives, we are empowered to face our pains, and Christ is able to heal us.

But the healing cannot take place unless you are willing to receive it. You must open your mind to the ideas that God wants to place there. You must be receptive to the work of the Holy Spirit within. The power of the Eternity Principle is released by your willingness to let God do his work within you.

The salvation of healing is to a large extent a re-inventing process. And it is not something that you do yourself, but rather something that you allow to be done. Relinquish control of your pain to God. Allow the life-giving flow of the Holy Spirit to wash through your mind, your spirit, and your body. When you allow this to begin, God is enabled to reach in and re-invent your thought patterns, release the power of life within you, and renew your mind, so that you begin to think the thoughts of Christ. And when you think his thoughts, salvation is inevitable. Because then you accept healing on his terms, by his definition, and you allow the Spirit to perfect you in the way that he chooses.

The Spirit of Christ is Life itself. Just as he invented our world, he now wants to re-invent our minds and spirits. As the Eternity Principle is activated within us, we are created all over again and we not only discover the unseen within us, but we see it as well.

Summary

The ultimate universal power is within your grasp, because it lives within you

**We choose to become
Spiritual Persons**

We discover the power of eternity by looking within ourselves and beyond ourselves

**In freedom we choose
The Eternity Principle
and release its power**

The Spirit
is Life Itself

Not only now,
but when I
reach God

~ St. Ignatius of Antioch ~

Book Three
Here and There

The Eternal World

Where is the Spiritual Realm? Many people imagine that the invisible world is light-years away. Since we are in the physical, seen world, and it is so very different from the eternal, unseen world, there is a contrived necessity for great distance between the two realities. But is it really that far from our temporal experience? In what I call the **Eternity Principle** we shall see that the two worlds are not far apart at all.

Our five senses (sight, hearing, touch, smell, taste) tell us of our environment. Anything beyond these physical responses, we feel, is at best far away, and at worst totally imagined. In our increasingly technological existence we reject any notion that some other reality might exist which the present human condition cannot detect. Simply put: In a world run by computers, where we have now unlocked the secrets of time and space, the myths of spirit and eternity are unwelcome intruders from a mystical past. Religion is only a crutch for as yet undeveloped cultures. Since we have entered a new age we must once and for all be done with tribal stories of gods and the realm of the spirit.

But does technology in fact negate the need for spiritual

sence? And if the unseen world is actually as real (maybe even more real) than the seen, should we disdain it simply because it escapes the sensations controlled by our brains? It is my conviction that a greater reality exists. It is an eternal reality that is invisible only to those who refuse to look for it. Further, it is not light-years hence. It is right here. Next to us. Within arm's reach. It is in fact a parallel dimension inhabited by God where spiritual things are just as real as physical things are to our own dimension.

Why has God chosen to hide this dimension from us? He has not deliberately hidden it – except to the extent that the unspiritual person is unable to believe in this greater reality. Further, God is a spiritual being and only spiritual persons can actually inhabit this eternal realm. Believers, then, are citizens of two worlds. On the one hand, we are the physical inhabitants of this dimension (including space, time, and the universe as we know it). On the other hand, we are citizens of the other dimension – the invisible world – because our spirits are joined with God through his Spirit. It is a simple concept on the surface, but a difficult idea to accept in a strictly physical, biological experience.

We enter the eternal world now. This is the idea that seems most baffling. Most people would admit that there is some possibility of an after-life. That is, we live this life and then far in a distant future we enter another world that is totally and completely separate from our own. To be sure, the realms of time and eternity are distinct. But they are not as far apart as we have always thought. The amazing fact is that God is very near. If your hand could breach the boundaries of the two dimensions, you could actually (right now) touch the spiritual world. It is that close. But the problem is that it is another dimension. It is parallel, yet separate.

How then, can we enter the eternal now? We can because the Eternity Principle has been activated in the minds of believers. The Apostle Paul calls this becoming a New Creature. In other words, at the moment of conversion something wonderful happens in the life of a Christian. He is ushered into a new reality. He is allowed to enter eternity and to experience the wonders of the spiritual realm. To be sure, Paul says that "now we see through a glass darkly, then face to face." But the fact remains that we actually see through the glass. The Holy Spirit literally brings our spirits (the Eternal within us) alive and the Eternity Principle is set into motion. It is a Principle which allows the believer to live in the here and now, and at the same time in the there and then.

Eternal Space

Why did God make a visible world and an invisible one in the first place? Why not have only one dimension where everyone can co-exist at once? It is because God is all spirit, completely eternal, and human beings are physical beings who are only partially spiritual. In addition, there was a necessity for separation because of the holiness of God. He is perfection and purity within personality. What is more, God is actually life itself. That is, the unimaginable power that it took to create the Universe is present within God.

It is impossible to wrap our minds around this concept. We have only an elementary understanding of the power and force necessary to create something from nothing. We say, "Oh, we created something." No. Perhaps we fashioned something or invented something, but we started with some other physical substance. In other words, we had something to fashion something else. God, on the other hand, actually *created*. That is, he took nothing – no substance – and made something from it. There were three things necessary for creation: God's incomprehensible imagination, which accounts for the wonder of the universe; God's immeasurable power, which accounts for something appearing where nothing had been before; and God's immutable will, which accounts for the fact that we are here.

So, God is in eternity and we are in time. Actually, we inhabit the dimensions of space *and* time. Although God inhabits these dimensions as well, it is because he chooses to inhabit them. God is not bound to these dimensions as we are. Instead, he inhabits that other dimension, eternity, which is spiritual and parallel to our physical dimensions. We live in time and then we die, both of which are very physical operations. Time itself is not physical, but it acts within the physical universe. God is not trapped in time as we are. He is above time. He is beyond the grasp of aging and death. He is not ruled by the setting and rising of the Sun as we are. He is other. He is eternal.

The miracle is that we can be eternal too. It is a choice, because we are not born with the Eternity Principle. It must be placed within us and activated by the Holy Spirit. But the glorious news is that in our freedom, of our own volition, we can choose to become eternal beings. When we accept Christ as Savior we are instantly made eternal persons. We escape the confines of space and time and actually – at that moment – enter Eternity. It is a mind-boggling concept, but one which is very real. Eternity is available for those who choose it. While remaining on in this world for the present, we are ultimately destined for eternity. For now we keep one foot in this dimension and one foot in the new dimension. But in the resurrection we will come to fully inhabit the spiritual, eternal realm. God did not have to invite us into his own private world. He was under no obligation to offer us the invisible citizenship. Still, the offer has been made and it remains valid for the twenty-first century. We live in the seen, but even now can view the unseen. We are here and there at once and God relates to us in both realities.

We have traditionally spoken of the transcendence and the immanence of God. In transcendence we have understood God to be far above us, completely separate, totally other. In immanence we have seen God as near to us, intimate, and one with us. The transcendent-immanent balance is a true picture of the way the Bible presents God to us. But we have misinterpreted transcendence. God is not far away in some unreachable land. While he is the Other and 'above' us in his holiness, he is not in some distant realm where he can only be reached by a cosmic long-distance operator. He is in another dimension, but it is a dimension that is here with us – right next door.

Following his resurrection, Christ made several appearances to his disciples. In some of those episodes, the early Christians were in locked rooms, when suddenly "out of nowhere" Jesus appeared. Where did he come from? Did he beam in from heaven by some kind of molecular-energy transporter system? Or did he, instead, simply step through a door? I think it was the latter. Christ appeared to his disciples by stepping out of eternity and back into time. He was never far away, only in a separate dimension. So, he did not have to travel light-years to once again fellowship with his followers. He simply opened the door to eternity, stepped through, and was once again visible in the dimension of space-time.

But citizens of the twenty-first century seemingly have no trouble with the nearness of spiritual things. Rather, we are finding it increasingly difficult to accept spiritual transcendence. I am not saying that God's existence, his holiness, his purity are not completely different from our human attempts at those attributes. God is spirit and he is eternal. My existence is dependent upon him, not the other way around. So we are not to lose sight of the quality of otherness about the divine. At the same time, though, we should not relegate God to some far-away planet where he can only spy on us through a cosmic telescope. To say that God is out of reach is equally wrong with saying he is my 'buddy.' God is near (just through the door, in fact), but he is holy in a way that we cannot even imagine and we are only made holy to some degree because of Christ and our relationship to him.

But holiness is available to us. And eternity is as well. We are here within time, but we can simultaneously experience the eternal realm through the avenue of the Holy Spirit. And with this experience of eternity comes personal, intimate contact with a holy being. Through this contact we are made holy. Now, we should not suppose that we are made equal with God, or that we attain holiness to the same degree as God. But we in fact participate in his holiness and become qualitatively different from our previous existence. In Christ we are holy and can enter the presence of God. Only holy beings or things made pure can coexist in the same dimension with God. He simply will not allow unholiness to come into contact with him. Since his holiness cannot be contaminated by communication with unholiness, and since we actually connect with divinity, we must of necessity have become holy.

Attainment of holiness is made possible through Christ. Because of his intimate contact with divinity, he is able to offer us divine communion. This communion is made real by the Eternity Principle. It is not that we somehow escape our bodies, or drift out of the here and now. Instead, divine communion and holiness are made available to us in our own dimension of space-time. For while we can see into eternity even now, we cannot fully enter that dimension until the resurrection. It is necessary, then, for eternity to be brought to us. Once again the door is opened. Once again a divine being is ushered through. And once again we are in the presence of holiness.

For now, however, it is not Christ himself who steps through the door. Rather, it is the Holy Spirit. In fact, the door has been left wide open and communication with God through the Spirit is an ongoing, continual opportunity. I remain here, but I can commune with him there. He resides there, but by his grace he offers himself to me here. The Here and There continuity of the Eternity Principle makes God real, not just in transcendence, but in a very intimate immanence.

Eternal Spirit

The indwelling of the Holy Spirit is a key factor in corresponding with the eternal sphere. There is a substance to spiritual things. They are not material, but nonetheless substantive. When the Spirit resides in the believer, there is an actual person there. To be sure, we do not experience the Spirit of God sensually, as we do our physical environment. Still, there is a *something* to the Spirit's indwelling. It is not just an idea, or some sort of nice philosophy. While the Spirit's presence is not physically tangible, it is spiritually tangible. Spirit has substance (although of a different nature) in the same way that material has substance.

So, when we are interacting with the eternal realm, we are engaging an actual, substantive place. It is an idea, but it is more. It is a theology, but it is more. The Spirit in reality connects us with eternity and draws the power of immortality within our bodies. Our spirits remain within us, yet are simultaneously projected beyond us into eternity. This is the power of the Eternity Principle. We do not leave the physical, biological, material world. And yet we do leave it. This mystery is at the heart of understanding how at once we are Here and There.

The Apostle Paul experienced this mystery. He tells us of being transported into the "third heaven" (2 Corinthians 12:2). Even at his recounting he remains unsure of whether it was a physical or purely spiritual experience. He is confident, though, that what he experienced was real. Paul had met Christ; he had spoken to him; he was There. And be sure of this, as well, that the eternal realm is not privy only to saints of the caliber of the Apostle. Instead, any believer is allowed access to the spiritual world. In fact, every person of spirit is specifically invited to enter the eternal.

We have, for example, the story of Solomon and his dialogue with God (1 Kings 3). Offered all the world's wealth, he chose instead the wisdom of God. In other words, told that he could live in luxury Here, he chose instead to connect with God There and begin living from a more eternal perspective. It was a simple request, yet for Solomon it was a life-changing question. "May I participate in your Wisdom?" became for Solomon a doorway into eternity. He was now able to use spiritual knowledge for practical, everyday tasks. The administration of an empire, although grandiose in scope, is actually rather mundane in practice. Yet to run an effective administration requires an almost superhuman amount of wisdom and a full database of knowledge. Solomon asked for these elements of eternity in his governance of Israel and was promised divine help and overall success.

Abraham is another biblical character who understood the power of the Eternity Principle. He had entered into a covenant with God in which the guarantee of spiritual assistance was one of the basic premises. As his story unfolds, we see a person who regularly employs faith in everyday living. Ultimately, he was willing to sacrifice his son (Genesis 22) in order for the Eternity Principle to be proven valid. The sacrifice, it turned out, was not necessary. What was requisite, however, was a complete trust in the divine/human relationship and the absolute assurance of mind that God would fulfill his promises.

Abraham was willing to take the risk to prove his faith and in the process the Eternity Principle became even more real for him than it had been before. And, in turn, his experience makes the Principle more real for us, too.

In our technological age, however, the application of the Principle can seem problematic. After all, we do not live in the agrarian world of biblical personalities. It may have been easy for them to accept the spiritual nature of eternity. In fact, a belief in eternity, particularly as a place, was probably easier to hold in a non-technical society. But how are we, as residents of a post-modern, post-literate, space age to integrate the reality of an eternal There with our scientific knowledge of a very present Here? Or, to put it more simply, are we obligated to believe in eternity just because primordial societies did?

To answer the question just as simply: No, we are under no obligation to accept the belief systems of ancient societies. In fact, there is a myriad of beliefs once held that we now reject out of hand. A flat earth as the center of the universe immediately comes to mind. At the same time, though, we should not automatically reject a belief simply because it was accepted as truth thousands of years ago. The belief in gods, for example, comes to us from time immemorial. Should we refuse to believe in a God or gods out of some sort of anti-ancient reflex? Or, instead, may we consider the matter on its own merits and then decide if it has a place in our own world?

Actually, even though some may still argue against the idea of a personal God, few will now argue against the existence of eternity. The plurality of beliefs now held worldwide all point, in some sense, to the reality of eternity. That is, at least as an idea. But what of eternity as a literal place? Notice I did not say a physical place, because eternity is not physical. It is not material (at least not as we understand material). Instead, eternity is a spiritual place, which is actually much more real than a physical place. But it does have dimension. Persons and objects do exist within that dimension. We can speak of eternity as a place because spiritual persons live within it. And persons, of necessity, need place (or dimension) within which to exist.

Eternal Kingdom

So, eternity is not just an idea. And it is not a formless void where disembodied spirits float somewhere between heaven and earth. Eternity is a spiritual place inhabited by spiritual persons. Some of those persons are now full citizens of that place. Others of us are only halfway citizens at present. That is because even though we have entered into eternity even now, we are also still Here. We are Here and There at the same time. But what we call Angels are living There as full citizens. God is There. That is not to negate the idea that God is everywhere. But if he is only everywhere, then he is nowhere. Persons cannot be everywhere, and as equally as God is deity, he is person. And as a person, God must inhabit place or dimension. It necessitates, then, that God lives in a place (eternity) and that while he is everywhere (Here), he is also not everywhere (There).

When Jesus taught about the Kingdom of God, he was quite clear that he was speaking of an actual place. To be sure, he taught that the Kingdom was a spiritual realm, but it was, for him, nonetheless literal. Christ's "Kingdom of God" or "Kingdom of Heaven" is equivalent to eternity. In both instances we are learning about an invisible, spiritual place that we can literally inhabit.

Christ is perfectly clear in the Sermon on the Mount (Matthew 5-7). The Kingdom is available. We are invited to enter it. The door has been opened wide. When faith is employed, the Eternity Principle suddenly appears on almost every page of Scripture. It is a spiritual principle that is understood and applied spiritually. Yet, it is also very practical in nature and can be set in motion with only a request.

In the Sermon, Christ talks about the Kingdom of Heaven. Specifically in the Beatitudes (or "Blessings") he gives several clues to becoming a citizen of eternity. He says first that the "poor in spirit" have a right to call eternity their own (Matthew 5:3). This may sound like a contradictory statement. When we think of entering eternity, we automatically picture spiritual wealth. In reality, according to Christ, the first step toward becoming a full-fledged citizen of eternity is to acknowledge the impoverishment of our spirits. That is, before the activation of the Eternity Principle, our spirits, having no life or power of their own, are poverty-stricken. We are "poor in spirit" and we must face our real condition in order to begin the process of coming to life.

Jesus also makes another seeming inconsistent statement. Not only will the spiritually poor enter eternity, but also those who are persecuted because they are exhibiting God's righteousness (Matthew 5:10). Persecution as a prerequisite to eternity does not sound very inviting. But notice his qualifier: it is because of righteousness. In other words, when we are rightly relating to God, indwelt by the Holy Spirit, and empowered by the Eternity Principle, we become citizens of his Kingdom. But with that positive promise comes a negative warning. Those who seek to live through Christ Here will encounter opposition and, perhaps, even persecution. It is proven history: when a person truly attempts to live by the Eternity Principle, she will almost certainly endure tribulation.

The point here, though, is that Christ is describing not just an idea, but an actual place. Eternity can be entered Here (partially), in anticipation of entering it There (completely). We are spiritual persons, brought fully alive by the Eternity Principle, and can reside in a spiritual realm. Still, we remain for now physical persons, who must continue to live Here and face the trials that life in a temporal world brings. Christ is the perfect example of a person who lived in both realms at once. While he was committed to his mission Here, he never allowed himself to forget the reality of There. He knew where his power came from. It was an eternal, internal, spiritual power, and Christ was fully aware that its source was from the other dimension, what he termed "the Kingdom."

Perhaps the idea of eternity as a literal place is even more transparent in Christ's conversation with a Jewish leader named Nicodemus. Nicodemus was intrigued by the teaching of Jesus and came to him privately to inquire more deeply about this new philosophy. In this dialogue, Christ again turns to the theme of the Kingdom (or eternity). He makes two lucid assertions that point unmistakably to the dimensional aspect of eternity. First, Jesus says, "unless a person is reborn he cannot *see* the Kingdom of God" (John 3:3, my emphasis). So, the Kingdom, or eternity, is a place that can be seen. But, as is usually the case with Jesus, there is a qualifier. In order to see the Kingdom, we must be "reborn." That is nothing except the activation of the Eternity Principle. When a person comes to know Christ in relationship, her spirit comes to life, her mind is enlightened, and she becomes a new person. In short, she is "reborn." And when such a relationship begins, the Eternity Principle is released within the spirit of the new believer, which then gives life and breath to this new birth.

So, after the Eternity Principle is triggered, we are able to literally see the Kingdom of God. We can perceive eternity. It is almost as if Christ is depicting a walled city. As we approach the city, we first see the outer walls, preventing our view into the interior. As we get closer, however, we can look through the gates and see into the city. At first we remain outside, but we can at least see in and begin to understand the dimensions, activity, and purpose of the city.

Christ's second assertion is even more to the point. After the Eternity Principle has begun to work within the new believer, and she can then see into eternity, she is then ready for the next step. "I am going to tell you an important truth," Jesus says. "Unless a person is born of water and born of the Spirit, he cannot *enter* the Kingdom of God" (John 3:5, my emphasis). Christ has already promised that we will see into eternity once the Principle has been activated. Now, he insists that we can enter eternity as well. Since it is impossible to enter somewhere that is not a place, Jesus affirms the dimensional aspect of eternity. The Kingdom is not just an idea, a mental attitude, or pious dreaming. Jesus is clear that his Kingdom is a place. We can see into this place, and we can enter it.

Again, Christ qualifies the entry. Not just anyone can walk up to the gates of eternity and saunter in. Only those who have been "born of the Spirit" are allowed admittance. Jesus is pointing to the Eternity Principle a second time. After the new birth, after we have come into relationship with him, we are given full citizenship in eternity. Think again of the walled city. We have walked up and seen the outer walls. At first we are unable to see within the city, but then we choose Christ and the Eternity Principle is engaged in our spirits. At that moment, we can see into eternity. We catch our first glimpse of the spiritual realm. We understand for the first time in our lives that there is something beyond our temporal existence. We accept and believe the reality of eternity, because we actually see into that dimension. We have turned to Christ and he has revealed himself to us.

But that is not the end of it, Jesus says. Citizens of the Kingdom are not forced to stand on the outside looking in. Rather, citizens enjoy full privileges within the city. We see eternity and then we enter into eternity. All of this, Jesus maintains, is made possible through the acceptance and practice of the Eternity Principle. The Holy Spirit is born within us, our spirits are made alive, and we enter into citizenship of God's Kingdom.

In the conversation reported in the Gospel of John, Nicodemus never seems to grasp what Christ is explaining. "I have been only describing the things of the earth," Jesus lamented. "How can you possibly believe if I were to explain heaven to you?" (John 3:12). If we cannot accept the reality of our temporal existence, how will we ever understand the greater reality of the spiritual realm? Some claim to believe in Here by denying the reality of There. "This is all there is," they seem to say. But this declaration denies the reality of our mysterious inner-selves. There really is more to humanity than meets the eye. But if we are unwilling to think through the simple things of this life, we will never begin to understand the much more complex issues of eternity.

But that is not a problem for persons practicing the Eternity Principle. We realize that the Principle is both propositional and dynamic. It is something we both accept as truth and practice as truthful. The Eternity Principle engages our spirits by the power of God's Spirit. It is within us. At the same time, though, we release the Eternity Principle through faith, so that we can become more Christ-like in our relationships. A person who enacts the Eternity Principle, then, is able to deal squarely with difficulties in life, because she believes in heaven. She has the strength to confront the realities of Here, solely because she is convinced of the reality of There. It is a place. It is real. And she has both seen and entered eternity and accepted full citizenship in the Kingdom.

With that citizenship, though, there are responsibilities. The Eternity Principle does not give us a free ride. The activation of our spiritual lives does not release us from responsibility, but actually enables us to see for the first time what our real responsibilities are. Certainly, there is freedom in the Kingdom. But true freedom always involves responsibility, because as a free person, alive in Christ, I will automatically care about your welfare and want the best for you, just as I want the best for myself.

Eternal Truth

People who accept the truth are attracted to the light, Christ said (John 3:21). When the Eternity Principle is activated within me, I accept the truth about my life Here and my potential There. I realize that I have limitations of talent and resources. But I also recognize the tremendous talents, and possibility of obtaining resources, that are available to me. The truth is that alone I am incapable of accomplishing very much of importance. But, my first step is to admit my impoverished state (Matthew 5:3). I accept the truth about my condition, but I also believe that through Christ my condition can be improved. The truth is that we do not have to remain impoverished. The truth is that we do not have to remain outside of the city. The truth is that we can accept the offer of life from Christ, allow his Spirit to occupy our spirits, and release the life-giving power of the Eternity Principle to address the problems of our lives Here.

As the Spirit of Christ infiltrates every part of our lives, we are drawn closer and closer to the light. Christ's truth shines within us and we can no longer accept those things about us that do not conform to his character. And this light is enlightening. My thought patterns begin to resemble ideas presented in Scripture. God's ideas become my ideas and solutions to problems are forthcoming. When I turn to the creator of the universe for solutions, I have gone to the very source of creativity. And problems are only opportunities waiting for a creative idea to take hold of them. Creativity, unleashed within my mind because of the Eternity Principle, turns my problems on their heads, shakes out the dust and shadows, and shines the light of Christ on them so that dilemmas are resolved and relationships are reconciled.

The Eternity Principle is propositional: it is a truth to believe and accept. It is also dynamic: it is truthfulness to put into practice in our lives. The responsibilities inherent in Kingdom citizenship can only be fulfilled through spiritual power. As we apply Christ's truth to our work and relationships, the Eternity Principle is transferred from our inner beings to our external world. We are able to fully enjoy our freedom in eternity, because we live up to our responsibilities and allow the light of Christ to shine through us to expose the darkness around us. As citizens of eternity, we do not turn within ourselves and lock out the needs that surround us. Like Christ, we face our world, uncover its untruth with our truthfulness, and display the power of the Eternity Principle so that others are attracted to the light. Our freedom is secure only insofar as we use liberty to procure it for others.

In the end, we realize that Here and There are not so far apart. The two dimensions are so close, in fact, that we are able to live in both at the same time. We see eternity and desire to enter it fully, but we recognize our obligation to help others see it and so we remain Here to fulfill our task. The full benefits of eternal citizenship await us There, but we are Here for now and are alive and well in both places.

Eternal Dialogue

How do we actually communicate with eternity? Since we have discovered that we can reach into the eternal dimension and connect our spirits with the divine spirit, is it then possible to carry on some level of discourse between the visible and invisible worlds? The answer, quite simply, is yes. Our contact with God does not end with some sort of cloudy spiritual feeling about the eternal realm. Instead, we can clearly communicate with eternity and come away with distinct ideas about how to use spiritual power in our lives. In short, we can both send and receive messages; and this kind of communication is usually referred to as prayer.

Prayer has both an inward and outward focus. I may be seeking answers to some problem and, in doing so, I not only ask for divine guidance, but I also ask questions of myself. Each of us is made in the image of God and born with a spark of his wisdom, his creativity, and his understanding. Then, after the Eternity Principle is mobilized, we have even greater access to the mind of God. So, prayer is not only an experience of seeking answers or help from without, but it is also a search within to uncover answers and help that already reside inside of us.

But prayer is more than meditation or contemplation. While meditation is a healthy spiritual practice, its focus is almost totally inward. In meditation I examine my own conscience, my own consciousness, and my own motives. I intensely look at myself and try to determine what steps I can take to become a more complete person.

Prayer, on the other hand, strikes a careful balance between the inner and the outer. To be sure, meditation is involved. I still examine myself. At the same time, however, I take a further step and seek out the mind of God. In other words, I reach into the invisible world, and by using the Eternity Principle, allow the thoughts and power of God to flow into me and add his creative solutions to my own. As a Christian, indwelt by the Holy Spirit, I need not depend solely on my own wisdom. I have the opportunity to obtain God's wisdom and apply his more perfect mind to whatever problem I am facing.

But if prayer is only a pious event which helps us to touch our inner selves, it is limited in scope and power. In fact, with that definition of prayer, there is actually no power except our own minds. For prayer to be really effective and meaningful, it must be connected to an outside source of power. That source is eternity, which contains the powerful force that created the universe. We are allowed, through prayer, to tap into the eternal, universal power source and use spiritual energy in our material world.

In thinking of prayer many people have developed a system whereby an objective entity called "prayer" produces cause and effect. They think that by somehow using the right formula that prayer, in and of itself, can miraculously make events or situations change. But the simple truth is that prayer doesn't change things. Instead, prayer changes people and people change things. Remember, the Eternity Principle allows you as a spiritual person to contact a spiritual person in the eternal sphere. And by virtue of that personal contact you are slowly changed and reformed into a complete human being. Prayer is the way you converse with God and by talking with him (and listening to him) the ongoing process is fueled with the divine energy necessary for this spiritual reformation and completion.

Prayer is the open-channel that allows communication between our world and eternity. Communication is always a two-way event. We speak to God – he listens to us. He speaks to us – we listen to him. It is sending and receiving. And the outcome is that we gradually become more like Christ. We begin to think with his thoughts and to address issues with his ideas. Through prayer the mind of Christ permeates my mind and I no longer rely on thought-patterns produced by the material world.

Instead, I am empowered by the creative thoughts of eternity, which, in turn, empower me to overcome the obstacles ahead of me.

If I have yet to master problems, it is because I still have not grasped the power that is offered to me. Do all of life's problems disappear because of the initiation of the Eternity Principle? Certainly not. In fact, some people will find there are more problems to deal with, simply because as spiritual persons they are now more aware of their surroundings. There is no magical solution to problems. But there are real solutions to them and the creativity to fuel those solutions is sent from eternity to the minds of believers. When we believe that answers are forthcoming, that act of faith throws open the doors of eternity and the ideas that are needed flow into our heads as surely as water flows over a fall. Conquering difficulties is well within God's providence and he is more than willing to send solutions to anyone willing to receive them.

Eternal Now

God lives above, or outside of, time. For God, it is always NOW. There is no past, present, or future in eternity, because God sees all things along our timeline at once. From the perspective of eternity, Julius Caesar speaking to the citizens of Rome, and Martin Luther King, Jr. proclaiming his dream in Washington, D.C. are both happening at the same 'time'. It is difficult for us to imagine, because we cannot picture reality apart from the dimensions of time and space. Caesar and Dr. King lived over two thousand years apart. But, for God, there is no 'this century' and 'that century'. It is just all *now*, since he is not bound by space and time as we are.

And so it is in prayer. As people throughout history are communicating with God, there is a wonderful harmony of voices penetrating eternity all at once. I think of St. Augustine, for example, as praying to God in the past. And I think of myself as praying to God today. But, in eternity, which exists apart from my idea of time, the prayers of Augustine and my prayers are received at once – because God can see all of human history at once.

This is why the prayers of past saints can actually bear upon your specific need. While Augustine cannot be praying for you in particular (he lived over fifteen hundred years ago), God can, if he chooses, receive Augustine's prayer on your behalf and act accordingly.

You can, for example, read a prayer of Augustine's that seems to fit your immediate need. You can simply ask God to hear that particular prayer of Augustine on your behalf. God is hearing the prayer of Augustine now and he is hearing your prayer now. If it sounds far-fetched, you have yet to free your mind from the bounds of time. We are talking about *eternity*. There is no 'time' and God can and does live in Now and sees all events of history simultaneously.

When you begin to understand this reality, it will make reading the prayer of Christ in John, chapter seventeen, truly exciting. In what we call *the high priestly prayer*, Christ petitions God on your behalf: "I have given to these believers the same glory that I received, so that they may participate in our perfect unity" (John 17:22). From our perspective, Christ offered his prayer two thousand years ago. But from the perspective of eternity, he is praying right now! Think of it, as you appeal to God today or tomorrow for his help with some problem, he hears your prayer and the prayer of Christ *at the same time*. In the mind of God, the Lord is bestowing on you his glory at the very moment of your request. And in that moment, the Eternity Principle becomes a powerful force in your life, because you are literally being pulled across the boundary of the eternal dimension by the prayer of Christ himself.

E.Y. Mullins in his classic work *The Axioms of Religion* (1908) introduces a term that shows the direct connection between the human and the divine in prayer. For Mullins, *soul competency* is the guarantee that each individual has the capability to reach God. By virtue of being human, created in the divine image, every person has an internal power which allows direct passage from the temporal to the eternal; from our world to God's kingdom. In the idea of soul competency we find a clear way to understand the possibility of entering the eternal realm through prayer.

In fact, Mullins insists in *Axioms* that each person has an inalienable right to one-on-one access to God. Soul competency, writes Mullins, "denies that there are any barriers to any soul to any part of the Father's grace." The notion that we somehow need a mediator to speak to God on our behalf simply will not do, Mullins says. Anticipating the theory behind the Eternity Principle by over one hundred years, Mullins shows how the internal spiritual energy which is generated by the divine/human connection actually, literally bridges the gap between the dimensions of time and eternity. Each of us is competent to speak to God. Each of us has the capability to not only reach out and touch eternity, but to enter into conversation with God and receive divine instruction for making our lives work here and now.

Mullins further explores this spiritual energy in his 1917 work *The Christian Religion in its Doctrinal Expression*. Here, the author lucidly explains the connection between the human in this dimension and the divine in the eternal dimension:

> *We know a power from without which has begun to act and continues to act within us. It is known as a power not previously in our consciousness. It sought us and found us. It is known to us as a spiritual power and we know the new power within us as personal.*

In this brief passage, Mullins points to all the major ideas within the Eternity Principle: The spiritual power comes from somewhere else (eternity); at one time we were unaware of the power, but now we possess it (activation); the power is alive in our consciousness and is actually connecting us to God spiritually (the Principle); and the power is not a nameless, faceless energy, but a person who relates to us individually and intimately (Christ).

Through the medium of prayer, we activate and reactivate the Eternity Principle as we continually connect with the spiritual realm in a very personal way.

Perhaps, though, the most exciting aspect of what Mullins believed, and in what I am telling you here, is that each of us has the potential for great personal power. Eternal energy is available for anyone who asks for it. This personal relationship with divinity is continuously offered and easily accepted. There are no tricks. There is no magic. It is the very simple process of receiving that which is being sent. The power to conquer every challenge in your life is within your reach. It's there for the taking. But, it must be received individually and internally.

The Eternity Principle is an inner power. While its origin is elsewhere (eternity), the way we contact this power is through our conscious minds. I send messages to God through prayer and God sends messages to me. God receives my communication and I in turn receive divine instructions. These instructions may be presented in the form of Scripture, inspirational writing or speaking, music, art, conversation, or personal thought. In any case, it is my mind, my consciousness, which is mobilized by the ideas I receive from God. I cannot think for you and you cannot think for me. Individually we choose to receive the inner power, to listen to the messages that are sent to us, and to change the direction of our lives because of spiritual guidance.

In short, the personal power that is available through prayer is exactly that – personal – and it must be received by individual choice.

Once the Eternity Principle has been activated within the believer, not only God's power, but also God's Spirit, takes up residence in the mind of the individual. In fact, it is the person of God, or Christ, that migrates from the eternal realm to the temporal and moves into the believer's consciousness. In other words, Christ's personality contacts and blends with the personality of each individual relating to him through the Eternity Principle. The personality of the believer is not annihilated, but it is certainly overwhelmed by the presence of this greater, eternal personality.

And so, when a believer prays to God, there is some sense in which God is communing with himself. In Romans, chapter eight, the Apostle tells us that our spirits meld with the Spirit of Christ. There is such a unity between the human and divine spirits, Paul says, that Christ's Spirit actually offers prayers for us. I once heard a retired missionary praying for someone ill. He said, "Lord, we are praying for Connie and we know that you are praying for her too." I like that. I am offering up a prayer, which in fact is Christ praying from within me. My spirit touches eternity at the same moment that the Spirit of Christ touches eternity. This human/

divine harmony transmits a spark of eternal energy right back into my mind, so that I am empowered to face and conquer all the challenges before me.

As human beings we are created in God's image. Then, after the Eternity Principle motivates our spirits to full life, Christ himself lives within us. When we pray to God, then, he is receiving a petition from himself. Remember that the mind of Christ is one of the foundational attributes of eternity. As his mind becomes my mind I begin to think (and pray) with greater clarity. Christ completely fills us by choosing to disperse himself beyond himself, so that while Christ is firmly seated in eternity, he is at the same time fully active in our world through us (Ephesians 1:23). God's image within us is given the full power of eternity and we are totally connected with the invisible realm by the personal presence of Christ within our minds.

Origen of Alexandria (third century CE) proclaimed that in prayer we stretch our minds to God. This is a certainty. But perhaps it is more exciting to realize that he is giving his mind to us. Our minds are reaching toward the mind of Christ and in touching, incredible power is released within us. Would it be too much to say that God is energized by this exercise as well? He chooses to reach out to us and to transfer his eternal energy into our temporal world. In so doing, he is connecting with something that is at the same time beyond himself and within himself. Christ fills everything, Paul says, and this divine permeation of all realms allows the eternal and the temporal to be in constant communication. We are energized by the touch of the eternal and Christ is energized because he is both sending and receiving the transmission.

When the Eternity Principle is initially activated, Christ is connecting with an individual in a brand new way. The divine mind then blends with the human consciousness to form a new symbiosis. After the initial contact, however, Christ reaches out from the eternal realm and connects with himself. He resides within the mind of the believer. He prays on behalf of the believer. His consciousness permeates the very being of the believer. In effect, Christ is sending himself a message from eternity. He receives this message (within our minds) and then inspires us to act in more effective ways.

It is truly glorious. We have been invited to become united with God. It is not just energy or power that is offered. It is not only creative ideas. It is more than mere answers to prayer. Instead, Christ offers us himself, his very person. And it is with his mind, and the continual influx of eternal energy, that I am able to face, and to facedown, all fears, worries, and problems that present themselves.

In prayer, you are doing more than seeking God. You are becoming one with God. Just think of it: your spirit fuses with Christ's Spirit and in that moment you have reached eternity. Sending petitions and receiving personality in an eternal circle of love, power, and unity.

Summary

The Eternity Principle enables us to live in the here and now with power and purpose

We can choose to release eternal creativity, so that we face any problem with God's ideas

Eternity is a place that we can see and enter into

We already enjoy the freedom of eternal citizenship

Our minds and the Mind of Christ are united in prayer to release a spiritual explosion of eternal power

Christ is praying for us in every moment of our lives

The soul
travels to
the invisible world

~ *Plato* ~

Epilogue

The Eternity Principle can help us make sense of our world and our place in it. The process of mind-renewal that is begun by the Eternity Principle leads to a greater awareness of our environment. Immediately we sense that we are no longer alone in the struggle. There is some power – some*one* -- who is beside us and within us to give us a clearer view of our problems and the available solutions for our souls. Maybe it isn't too much to say that *soulutions* are there for the asking.

So many people wander through life with few ideas about how to conquer challenges. For them, it seems that life is the enemy and they are always on the losing side. Such people focus on the problems, not the solutions; on the negative, not the positive; on themselves, not God. It really is sad, because the voice of God is strong and clear. It calls across time, across racial and gender borders, across class structure, and across cultural barriers. The voice is an invitation to become one with God and the invitation is always extended.

There are other people who hear the call and accept the invitation. They understand the relationship between time and eternity. They have seen into the unseen world and have an unobscured vision of their personal futures. The Eternity Principle has become active for these persons and now eternity is more than an idea. Eternity is a reality. And tomorrow has endless possibilities because there are endless tomorrows that await them.

If the Eternity Principle remains for you simply a term or an unfocused theory, the power that is readily available will continue to be just out of reach. On the other hand, if you begin to see the Eternity Principle as the literal, actual presence of God within you, then divine energy is already enthusing you and you are prepared for anything life presents.

While the invisible realm of eternity will remain invisible to many people, you are now prepared to open your spiritual eyes and see into Christ's kingdom. Christ has promised that once we see eternity, we are then able to enter in, to be reborn, and to become united with him in our minds and spirits. The invitation to enter is graciously given and can, at any moment, be personally received.

There is no longer any reason to doubt: Eternity is real and can be experienced. The Eternity Principle liberates your mind to accept this reality and energizes your consciousness to understand it. Amazing, isn't it? Eternity was right here all along.

Thank You

- Members of the Historical Society for your unswerving belief in our mission.
- DCHS Board of Trustees for your continuing devotion to our mission.
- DCHS Staff for the sacrificial service you provide to everyone interested in our history.
- Marlene Patterson for keeping me on time in all my travels.
- Kristin Russell for your excellent design work on this and many projects. YATB.
- Alvin Jackson for your encouragement and kindness.
- Leslie and Will for sharing your lives and love with me and making me very proud of my family. You are the proof that I am blessed.

The Eternity Principle
by Glenn Thomas Carson
and many other titles
available at
www.PolarStarPress.com

POLAR STAR PRESS
† ✦